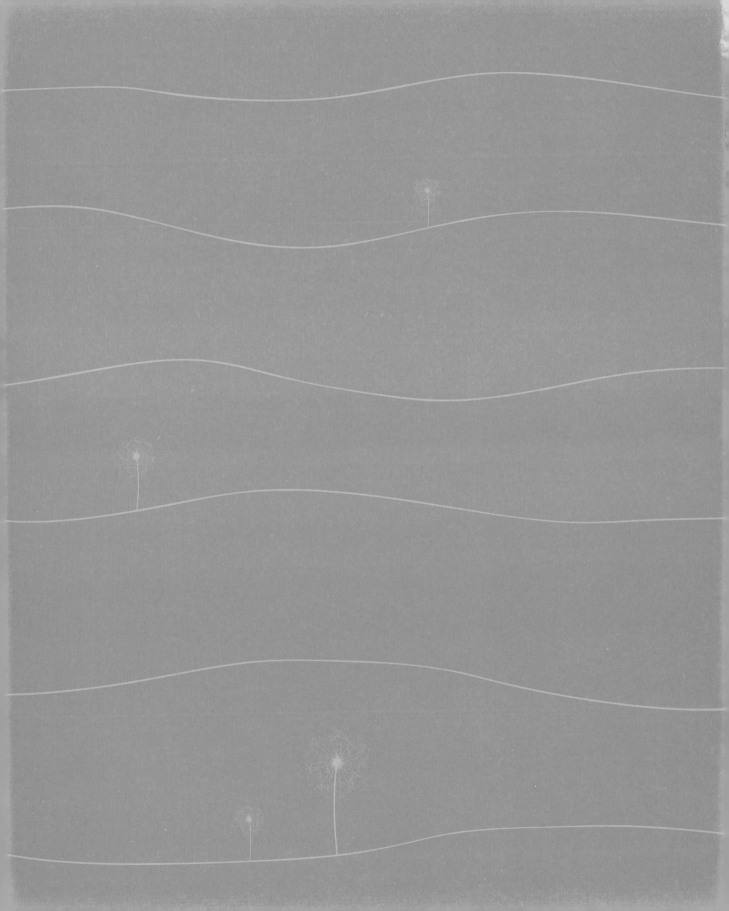

ORCA FOOTPRINTS

Save Our Seeds

PROTECTING PLANTS FOR THE FUTURE

SHERYL NORMANDEAU

ORCA BOOK PUBLISHERS

Published in Canada and the United States in 2024 by Orca Book Publishers.
orcabook.com

Library and Archives Canada Cataloguing in Publication
Title: Save our seeds : protecting plants for the future / Sheryl Normandeau.
Names: Normandeau, Sheryl, author.
Series: Orca footprints.
Description: Series statement: Orca footprints ; 31 |
Includes bibliographical references and index.
Identifiers: Canadiana (print) 20230457916 | Canadiana (ebook) 20230457975 |
ISBN 9781459836976 (hardcover) | ISBN 9781459836983 (PDF) |
ISBN 9781459836990 (EPUB)
Subjects: LCSH: Plant conservation—Juvenile literature. |
LCSH: Seeds—Protection—Juvenile literature.
Classification: LCC QK86.A1 .N67 2024 | DDC j333.95/316—dc23

Library of Congress Control Number: 2023939044

Summary: Part of the nonfiction Orca Footprints series for middle-
grade readers, illustrated with photographs throughout, this book
examines the importance of seeds to all living things, the threats they
face and why we have to preserve and conserve seeds for the future.

Orca Book Publishers is committed to reducing the consumption of
nonrenewable resources in the production of our books. We make
every effort to use materials that support a sustainable future.

Orca Book Publishers gratefully acknowledges the support for its publishing
programs provided by the following agencies: the Government of Canada,
the Canada Council for the Arts and the Province of British Columbia
through the BC Arts Council and the Book Publishing Tax Credit.

Front cover photos by (top) TinnaPong/Shutterstock.com;
(bottom) Léa Jones/Stocksy
Back cover photo by HMVart/Getty Images
Design by Troy Cunningham
Edited by Kirstie Hudson

Printed and bound in South Korea.

27   26   25   24   •   1   2   3   4

Seeds are plants-in-waiting.
SHOWCAKE/GETTY IMAGES

To Rob, Mum and Dad, and Derek,
with all my love.

Contents

CHAPTER ONE
WHY ON EARTH ARE SEEDS SO IMPORTANT?

CHAPTER TWO
HUMAN INTERVENTION

CHAPTER THREE
ENVIRONMENTAL CHALLENGES

CHAPTER FOUR
SEEDS FOR THE FUTURE

Introduction

Here I am surrounded by flowers and seeds in a wild space in the mountains— one of my favorite places to be!
ROB NORMANDEAU

I live in the foothills of the Rocky Mountains, and every July I try to go on at least one hike when the wildflowers are in bloom. The sight of meadows filled with color—paintbrush, shooting stars, calypso orchids and buffalo beans—is breathtaking. (Not to mention extremely exciting for the bees that buzz around the flowers!) These flowers grow each year and spread abundantly over the ground because their seeds are moved around by wind or by mammals and birds.

As I marvel at the views in the mountains, I think about the importance of seeds. Seeds provide us with food, clothing, wood and other materials. Flowering plants reproduce by seeds. Without seeds, the planet wouldn't have as many species of plants as we do now. That would affect human life as well as wildlife and insects, which rely on the plants that grow from seeds for habitat and food.

Yet seeds are under threat, mostly from human activity. Factors such as the climate crisis and food-security issues mean

that it is more important than ever to save seeds for the future. Governments and global organizations are coming together to try to protect and preserve seeds, but we also need to do our part.

Every spring I plant seeds. I live in an apartment, so I have only a small balcony and a plot in a nearby community garden in which to grow my garden. I grow vegetables and herbs for myself and my husband, and to share with my family and friends. Over time I have taught myself how to save seeds properly, so that they are useful for planting the next year. I save as many seeds as I can—far more than I can possibly plant in my tiny garden—and I share them with anyone who wants them. Other seeds, such as those from the sunflowers I grow, are left in the garden as energy-rich treats for the birds.

On my own, I can't do a lot, but think about it—each tomato seed will grow a single plant that can produce hundreds of seeds from the tomato fruit it bears! If I can save most of those seeds, I can grow more tomato plants next year and help many other gardeners grow tomato plants of their own. If the gardeners I help also save their seeds, and so on, we can make a bigger impact. Are you ready to find out why seeds are so important and learn how to save seeds of your own? Let's head into the garden.

The world's smallest seeds are from a type of orchid. They are smaller than most particles of dust. And what about the world's largest seeds? If you guessed that they come from a species of coconut, you'd be correct. No matter what size they are, seeds are potentially full of life.
ELENA MEDOKS/GETTY IMAGES

Many people who live in large cities do not have a lot of space for growing a garden. But even if you have only a container or two of plants, you can still save seeds.
ISA LONG/SHUTTERSTOCK.COM

CHAPTER ONE

Why on Earth Are Seeds So Important?

10 Types of Seeds

There are so many different types of seeds!

- CLOVE
- COCONUT
- COFFEE BEAN
- CORN
- MUSTARD
- PEA
- PEANUT
- PINE NUT
- PISTACHIO
- QUINOA

Can you name other plants that have seeds?

WHAT IS A SEED?

A seed is a baby plant waiting to happen. Inside a seed is a *fertilized embryo*. A special casing called an **endosperm** is wrapped around the embryo. The endosperm contains all the energy a seed needs to **germinate**. The outer part of the seed is called the **testa**. This coating protects the seed until it is time for it to produce a plant. When the seed is given oxygen, water and the right temperature to sprout, it will expand, and the little shoots will burst forth through the seed coat. We store seeds in a cool, dry place to keep them from sprouting when we don't want them to. When we're ready to plant them, we give them the water, air and conditions they need to "wake up."

WHAT'S YOUR SEED TYPE?

There are many different types of seeds, including **heirloom**, open-**pollinated** and **hybrid**. To save seeds successfully, we need

BEAN SEED

Testa

First leaves

Hilum

Epicotyl

Hypocotyl

Radicle

Endosperm

WHOLE

CROSS SECTION

Let's take a look at a bean seed in more detail:

The **radicle** is the part of the germinating seed that pushes deep into the soil to start the plant's root system. The **first leaves** are attached to the **hypocotyl**, which is the stem of a germinating seed. The **epicotyl** is the growing tip of the hypocotyl. It helps the stem of the seed push up out of the soil. The **endosperm** is the special casing around the seed embryo and the **testa** is the outer part of the seed. The **hilum** is a mark on the outside of the seed that shows where it had been attached to the plant it came from.

to know what types we are growing. Some of them are not ideal for saving, and others are just right.

Heirloom and Heritage

These are seeds that have been passed down from generation to generation. We save the seeds of plants such as Paris Market carrots or French Breakfast radishes, grow them, then save more seeds from the new plants. Some heirloom seeds have been passed down for centuries. In the late 18th century, the seeds of a delicious squash were brought from the West Indies to the United States. In 1842 a gardener named Elizabeth Hubbard shared some of her saved squash seeds with neighbor James Gregory. He named the plants after her. The seeds continued to be shared year after year, and we still grow Hubbard squash today. When it comes to seeds, the labels *heirloom* and *heritage* mean pretty much the same thing.

Healthy plants come from healthy seeds. It is important to know that the seeds you are planting do not have any diseases. The seeds should have been saved from plants that were strong, not sickly and weak.

Open-Pollinated Seeds

Open-pollinated (OP) seeds are pollinated by insects or the wind. OP seeds are saved because they grow into plants with delicious flavor, color or some other **trait** we love. Many heirloom seeds, such as Blue Lake bush beans, are also OP seeds because they're pollinated by bees. OP seeds that are grown in a certain region can usually adapt to the climate there.

Heirloom tomatoes have interesting shapes and colors—and they taste amazing!

Knowing what type of seed you are growing is a must when it comes to properly saving it for the future.
SHERYL NORMANDEAU

Hybrid

Hybrid seeds are created by ***crossbreeding*** two different varieties of plants. The amount of food harvested from hybrid plants is often larger than from OP plants. They are bred to produce bigger yields.

The seeds of hybrid plants will not grow into plants that are the same as their parent plants. The seeds will grow into a new plant with different traits. If you are saving seeds, choose OP seeds instead of hybrids. Plants grown from OP seeds will be the same as their parent plants. If you like the way that those Blue Lake beans taste and look, you want to be sure that the seeds you saved from them grow into plants that have the same flavor and appearance.

Hybrid vegetables won't always taste as good as heirloom ones. This is because they are bred for other traits, such as the ability to be stored for a long time. Hybrid vegetables are usually found in supermarkets because they can be transported better than heirloom veggies.

WHAT WOULD LIFE BE LIKE WITHOUT SEEDS?

Without seeds and the plants that grow from them, life would be very difficult for all living organisms on earth. Plants provide us with food, medicine, fibers for clothing and other materials, such as wood and fuel. They are food and habitat for wildlife and livestock, and in turn humans eat some of these animals for food. Think about all the interactions with plants you have

When you get your garden ready for winter, do not cut off the seed heads of your plants. Many bird species are seed eaters, and they will be happy for the food.
BOUKEATEMA/GETTY IMAGES

before you even get to school in the morning! The clothes you put on may have been dyed with plants. The orange juice you drink and the flakes of the cereal you eat are made from plants. The minty flavor in your toothpaste comes from a plant.

SEED MONEY

In the past some seeds were so important that they were valued as money. The Maya were not the first culture to harvest the seeds (called beans) of the cacao tree in the area of Mesopotamia we now call Mexico. (The Mokaya began saving seeds before the Maya, around 1000 BCE.) But the Maya were the first to treat the seeds of the cacao tree as a form of payment. The beans were also part of ceremonies that celebrated big life events. Between 691 and 900, cacao beans (and a hot chocolate-flavored drink made from them) were used in wedding ceremonies and baptisms. Emperors saw the seeds as **status symbols**, and when they died they were buried with jars filled with cacao beans. Workers were even paid with cacao beans, and the beans were used to pay for clothing and food and given as gifts and offerings to the gods. When the Maya started trading with the Aztecs around 1400, the Aztecs accepted cacao beans as a tribute. The practice continued for hundreds of years.

Sow Deeper: Traditional Medicine Plants?

Indigenous Peoples all around the world have been using plants for medicine for thousands of years. The Anishinaabe in what are today known as western Quebec and Ontario use the roots and buds of balsam poplar to make a salve to heal the skin. In Canada more than 400 different types of plants have been used by Indigenous Peoples in the past—and many are still in use by them today. These plants help people recover and heal from health problems, and some prevent some sicknesses. Skilled healers are trained to know how to harvest, prepare and give medicines. They have respect for the plants that give medicine and treat them as relatives.

GENERATION TO GENERATION

Seeds that have been passed down from generation to generation are reminders of the people who lived before us, who planted crops and gathered the harvest. Sometimes seeds are shared in unexpected ways. Seeds from the original Black Krim tomato plants were brought back to Britain, Italy, France and Türkiye by soldiers fighting in the Crimean War (1853–1856). Gardeners liked the way the tomatoes tasted and looked, and they continued to save them and share them with others all over the world. Because of this, we still grow Black Krim today.

The Cultural Importance of Seeds

Seeds also represent places and cultures. Mexico is known for its spicy hot peppers, such as the poblano, habanero and jalapeño. When we grow these peppers in our own gardens—no matter what part of the world we are living in—we know where they originated, and we enjoy them in meals that are inspired by Mexican culture. Think about your own heritage. What types of seeds would your ancestors have grown? What kinds of plants would they have eaten?

SURVIVAL OF THE SPECIES

All the different varieties of life on Earth—from microscopic one-celled organisms to gigantic mammals such as whales—make up the *biodiversity* of our planet. Plants are a critical part of this biodiversity. All living organisms are connected in this web of life. For example, native leafcutter bees help pollinate alfalfa,

Planting only one type of plant in your garden is called monoculture. (Mono means "one.") Planting lots of different varieties is a good way to have a biodiverse garden. Look at all the different types of gourds you can grow!
(TOP) VGAJIC/GETTY IMAGES;
(BOTTOM) EYEWOLF/GETTY IMAGES

which is an important crop that humans feed to livestock such as cattle. If bee populations are reduced by disease, pesticides or extreme weather, the alfalfa won't be pollinated. That means the plants won't produce the seeds people need to grow the next crops of alfalfa. Without more alfalfa, they will lose that food for cattle. That, in turn, means the cattle cannot be raised for meat and milk. It also means a key part of the economy is lost.

Researchers have found that three species of plants each year since 1900 have become extinct and that one-fifth of the world's plants are in danger of extinction. If too many plants become extinct due to the climate crisis or some other catastrophe, plant diversity will be affected. We will lose species of plants that are needed for food, medicine or other uses. Wildlife and insects that rely on plants for food and habitat may also be lost. This will impact human life too. It's easy to see how important it is for us to encourage biodiversity in the world. Saving seeds is one way to do this.

Have you ever noticed how fuzzy bees are? When a bee lands on a flower, pollen sticks to the hair on its body. Some species of bees have a tiny pollen basket on each of their back legs. They can store pollen in the baskets while they fly around.
QNITA/GETTY IMAGES

PROPAGATION EXPLORATION

When plants produce seeds, this is called *sexual reproduction*. For seeds to be made, the flower must be fertilized. But plants can also reproduce in other ways. When a gardener takes a

There are many ways to make new plants. The strawberries in this photo were grown from seeds. The pothos plants in the far left of the picture are cuttings that are being rooted in water.
OSTANINA ANNA/SHUTTERSTOCK.COM

cutting of a plant, they are making a new plant by way of asexual (or vegetative) reproduction. I have a beautiful houseplant called an African violet. I can take a leaf cutting from it and let it grow roots by putting it into soil. Eventually that single leaf will grow into another African violet plant that is identical to my original one.

Grab a banana and peel it, then take a bite. Did you eat any seeds? Nope! That's because the bananas we buy in grocery stores in North America are not grown from seeds. They are seedless varieties that humans have bred. Bananas grow on trees that have many stalks branching out from a main stalk. Once the tree has produced fruit, all but the main stalk die. Side shoots, called suckers, grow out of the base of the main stalk. Banana growers remove the suckers and plant them to get more banana trees—and fruit!

The More the Better

Another way we can reproduce plants without using seeds is through a method called *tissue culture*. A small part of the plant is cut and grown in a container filled with a liquid solution of nutrients. Companies that grow plants for the **horticultural** industry might use tissue culture because they need to grow thousands of identical plants to sell to customers.

If we can grow plants in a **petri dish** or by taking cuttings off plants we already have, why are seeds so important? Earlier I mentioned that any plants grown by asexual reproduction are **clones** of the parent plants. Instead of 10 different varieties of African violet, you have 10 copies of one African violet. That's bad, because if there are only a few plant varieties, they could be wiped out instead of adapting to the climate crisis or resisting **pathogens** and pests. The more varieties of plants there are in the world, the better they can adapt. Seeds are the key to encouraging plant diversity in the world.

Sow Deeper: What about Plants That Don't Flower?

Did you know that some plants do not naturally produce seeds? Ferns, liverworts and mosses don't—they reproduce with spores instead. If you've ever been hiking in a marsh, you may have seen horsetails. The ancestors of these interesting nonflowering plants were found in fossil deposits 325 million years ago—and our modern horsetails haven't changed much since!

GOOD CHARACTER

Saving seeds makes you part of history. For example, you might be growing a tomato plant. You like everything about this plant—the delicious, sweet fruit, the nice short height of the plant and the way it seems to grow well in the clay soil you have in your garden. These are all traits you want more plants to have, making this a good tomato plant from which to save seeds. Those seeds should produce plants that have the same traits as the parent plant.

Humans have been saving seeds for 12,000 years. Once our ancestors figured out that they could settle in one place and grow their own food instead of roaming around hunting and gathering, they needed to save seeds to keep their crops growing from year to year. They also needed to save seeds to keep making their crops better and more resistant to pests and diseases, and producing tastier food. This is called *selective breeding*. You can do the same things as those early humans did thousands of years ago by saving the seeds from the healthiest plants in your garden.

This is the spore-producing stage of a horsetail. After the spores are released, the plant sends up green stems with bristly green branches.
SHERYL NORMANDEAU

CHAPTER TWO

Human Intervention

SEEDS ARE BIG BUSINESS

In the past no one owned seeds. Seeds were available for everyone to save and share and sow. Eventually seeds were collected and packaged by seed companies to be sold in stores. Although the seed companies and the stores had an inventory of seeds, they couldn't tell a gardener or farmer not to save the seeds of the plants they grew. The companies and stores couldn't prevent someone from breeding new plants by selecting the best seeds from the plants they grew. Not restricting the way that seeds were saved or used to breed better plants meant that farmers and gardeners could increase biodiversity.

THOSE ARE MY SEEDS

Over the past few decades, governments around the world have put laws into place that allow some plant breeders and large corporations to *patent* certain seeds and plants. This means those

These women are packing seed envelopes in the early 1900s. After they place five seeds inside each envelope, they put it on an assembly belt, and the packet is moved down the line.
LIBRARY OF CONGRESS/WIKIMEDIA
COMMONS/PUBLIC DOMAIN

breeders and corporations own the seeds. It is illegal for farmers and gardeners to save seeds from those plants and sell or share them. Everyone must buy new seeds from the corporations and the breeders when they need them. The corporations and the breeders make money from sales of their seeds. Many patented seeds come from agricultural crops such as soybeans and wheat.

Some corporations own thousands of patents on plants. They can increase the price of seeds when they wish, meaning some people may not be able to afford them. Farmers and gardeners might not be able to grow their own food. It also means that there are fewer varieties of seeds to choose from. This affects the biodiversity of our whole planet. The more varieties of plants we have in the world, the more likely they are to adapt to climate change and pests and diseases.

In this automated seed-packaging system from the early 1900s, seeds are dropped down a chute from the upper floor of the factory. Machines automatically open the empty packets, and the seeds are poured inside.
LIBRARY OF CONGRESS/WIKIMEDIA
COMMONS/PUBLIC DOMAIN

The next time you transplant a plant into a new pot or garden bed, think about how that seed you put into the soil has grown into a plant that is now big enough to move out of its small pot and into a new home. Transplanting will allow the roots to grow bigger, and the plant will grow taller and wider.
LYONA/SHUTTERSTOCK.COM

INVASIVE PLANT ALERT!

Sometimes the trading and movement of plants across the world can be a good thing. In the 16th century Spanish colonizers discovered potatoes in South America and eagerly brought them back to Europe. A few decades later, Europeans then brought potatoes to North America, where we enjoy them now. (What would life be like without french fries or mashed potatoes?) European colonizers were also responsible for bringing the seeds for crops such as wheat to North America.

But when seeds are moved from one part of the world to another, the result isn't always good. The human transport of seeds can bring *invasive* species to a new land, and it can cost a lot of money, labor and time to control or remove the invasive plant from its new home.

Kudzu has been known to grow as much as a foot (30 centimeters) each day! No wonder it can take over an area so quickly.
ROBERTO MICHEL/SHUTTERSTOCK.COM

Taking Up Space

What makes a plant invasive? Invasive plants are nonnative plants that cause harm to other plants, livestock, pets, wildlife and humans. They are introduced to a new place when humans collect, move and plant seeds or other parts of plants, or when animals and wind disperse the seeds. Kudzu is one of the most invasive plants in the southern United States, but it was deliberately brought from Asia in the 1930s to help control soil erosion.

When invasive plants are introduced to a new environment where they have the right growing conditions, they can multiply and spread quickly. That means they can compete with **native** plants for nutrients, water, sunlight and space, crowding them out. This reduces biodiversity in an area. Or, because there are so many of them, the invasive plants might be resistant to diseases and pests, giving them a better chance of survival than the native plants have. Some invasive plants are toxic to humans, livestock and wildlife. Some can destroy habitat, such as waterways or pastures where livestock graze. This can affect the economy by harming industries such as forestry, agriculture and fisheries. Our food supply can even be threatened. For example, if pastures are destroyed by invasive plants, ranchers will not be able to raise cattle or other livestock that we rely on for meat and other food products.

Instead of being sprayed with chemicals and herbicides, invasive plants are often pulled by hand. This can be hard work and take time, but it is more environmentally friendly.
JUSTIN SCOTT NPS

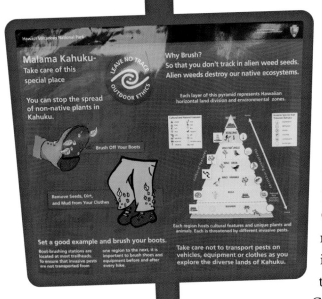

WEED CONTROL

Governments work to keep invasive plant species from harming the environment and causing problems for trade and commerce all over the world. Many countries have laws to prevent invasive plants from being bought, sold, transported, planted and allowed to spread. In the United States and Canada, the federal and state or provincial governments create and enforce these laws. One of the most important things the federal government does is ensure that invasive plants are not brought into the country when goods are imported (or shipped to other countries with exports). In the United States, Customs and Border Protection agents who specialize in the biological sciences and agriculture check for invasive species of insects and plants in baggage, trucks and containers coming into the country from a foreign source. Agents are sometimes helped by detector dogs trained to sniff out such plants and pests.

Most provinces in Canada have their own version of a weed-control act, which is a legal document used to manage invasive plant species. The United States has the Federal Noxious Weed Act, put into law in 1975. Weed inspectors check for invasive plants on farm- and rangelands, in home gardens and at places of business. If a weed inspector finds invasive plants on a property, they can fine the owner. We all have a responsibility to keep invasive plants from spreading—and that means we must stop the seeds of those plants from moving around.

Black henbane is a common invasive species found in many areas of Canada. A single plant can produce up to 500,000 seeds each year. And because it is poisonous, it is especially important that it doesn't grow in fields where livestock graze.
(TOP) NPS PHOTO/S. GEIGER;
(BOTTOM) SHERYL NORMANDEAU

Sow Deeper: Wipe Your Feet!

If you travel to Waterton Lakes National Park in Alberta, you'll see boot-brush stations at many trailheads. Before and after hiking the trail, hikers must wipe their boots on a brush built into a special rack. This helps prevent knapweed seeds and other invasive plant species from spreading into new areas of the park. It's one way Parks Canada is trying to control the invasive plant from harming other plants in this delicate ecosystem.

THE STORY OF A MAIL-ORDER SEED SCHEME

In the summer of 2020, hundreds of people in Canada and the United States found mysterious envelopes in their mailboxes. The envelopes contained seeds from unknown plant species, and they were sent from China or Taiwan. The people who received the seeds had not purchased them. The Canadian Food Inspection Agency (CFIA) and the United States Department of Agriculture (USDA) quickly asked people not to plant the seeds. The danger was that the seeds could be from invasive plants that would be harmful if introduced to North America. There was also a risk that the seeds could be infected with a seed disease or even bring in an insect pest from another continent. The CFIA and the USDA asked people who had received seeds to send them to their country's government agency for testing.

It's easy to see from this example how potentially harmful seeds can be transported and spread. If just one gardener received the mystery seeds and planted them—and if the seeds were from an invasive species—they could create a huge problem in the long term.

To ship seeds internationally, you must follow certain rules. Check the seeds regulations on your federal government's website for more information about shipping and receiving seeds internationally.

As for the mystery seeds sent from China and Taiwan? Government agriculture departments in Canada and the United States tested them and found out the seeds were not dangerous. Most were for plants commonly grown in North American gardens, such as mint, cabbage and mustard. The light, inexpensive packages were likely mailed out by companies that wanted to get reviews on online shopping websites. Even though the seeds turned out to be harmless, the mail-out was still illegal because they were sent to North America without having the proper permits.

SEED-PROTECTION LAWS AND FAKE SEEDS

In Canada, the Seeds Act came into effect in 1923. In the United States, there is the Federal Seed Act, created in 1939. These acts ensure that the seeds purchased by farmers to grow on their land are of high quality. They should not have diseases, for example, and most should be guaranteed to germinate. The seeds must have been stored properly before they were purchased so the farmer does not have to worry about them going bad before they are planted. They must also be labeled clearly to say what type of plant they are from and where and when they were collected.

In some parts of Africa, the trade of illegal seeds, called *seed fraud*, is causing huge problems for farmers. When they buy seeds for their farms from suppliers in their own countries, they expect to receive high-quality seeds that

Knowing where seeds come from and whether they are of high quality is very important to farmers.
BLOOMBERG CREATIVE/GETTY IMAGES

will germinate well and be disease-free. But in many cases, the seeds are actually of poor quality. They might be old or have been stored improperly. The labels might be wrong or have been changed. Some suppliers are trying to make bigger profits by selling bad seeds, even though it is against the law to do so.

There are fears that these illegal seeds could lead to crop failures and food shortages. To try to fight seed fraud, some suppliers are selling certified seeds that have been tested, but they are more expensive than other seeds. Many of the farmers are poor and cannot afford the certified seeds, but they have no way of knowing if the cheaper seeds are of high quality.

Gardeners who don't have large gardens like having the choice of growing small plants that fit their space. Selective breeding helps make this happen.
SHERYL NORMANDEAU

Bacillus thuringiensis (Bt) can kill all species of Lepidoptera, including this beautiful fritillary butterfly found in northern Alberta.
TINA BOISVERT

GM AND GE SEEDS: IT'S COMPLICATED!

Remember our ancestors who started farming and gardening 12,000 years ago? While they were selectively breeding plants for the useful traits they wanted to keep, they were actually changing the **genetics** of the plants they were growing. Selective breeding is a form of genetic modification. One of my favorite varieties of tomatoes, called Extreme Bush, is genetically modified (GM). It was selectively bred so the plants would only grow to be about 23 inches (60 centimeters) tall. It's the perfect tomato for my small balcony!

Do you know what carpology is? No, it's not the study of a certain type of fish. It's the study of seeds and fruits. Carpologists focus on understanding their structure, or form, and how it works.
MINT IMAGES/GETTY IMAGES

Genetic Engineering

Genetic engineering is different from genetic modification. Over the past few decades, researchers have figured out a way to combine genes from two different **kingdoms**. For example, they can put part of the genetic material from a bacterium called *Bacillus thuringiensis* (Bt) into plants such as cotton and corn. Bt is found naturally in the soil. Certain proteins from Bt can be used as an insecticide, which can prevent many types of caterpillars from eating plants.

Although these genetically engineered (GE) seeds are tested, and many countries' governments allow them to be grown legally on farms, some people think that combining genes from two different kingdoms is a bad idea. They think the plants grown from the seeds might be harmful to eat. They are not sure if humans should be tampering with nature when the consequences of doing so are unknown. In Canada, a small number of genetically engineered crops are grown on farms, but as of 2022, no GE seeds were collected and sold for use in home gardens.

Scientists do experiments to find out such things as whether a seed needs light or darkness to germinate, how long seeds can be stored and still sprout, and how to breed plants that taste better or can handle hot or cold weather.
NOEL HENDRICKSON PHOTOGRAPHY/
GETTY IMAGES

CHAPTER THREE

Environmental Challenges

FACT

Scientists have determined that the amount of greenhouse gases trapped in Earth's atmosphere is at its highest level in two million years. Since 1880 the planet has warmed by about 2°F (1.1°C). Most of that temperature increase has happened since 1975. This is a huge change in a very short period of time.

Can you imagine what removing all these trees does to the environment? This photo shows a heavily logged area in northern Alberta, but deforestation is happening on this scale all over the planet. It significantly alters global climates.
ROB NORMANDEAU

FACING THE CLIMATE CRISIS

The climate crisis is causing many problems on our planet. Warmer temperatures are creating longer growing seasons in some regions. Insect pests are moving across the planet into new habitats. The warming temperature in the northern hemisphere means that insects from other regions can now survive in a climate that was once too cold for them. For example, the Canadian government is working to keep the spotted lanternfly from moving into the country from the United States. Newcomer insects like these eat plants that humans need for food. They have no natural predators in their new homes, which means they quickly increase in number. The changing climate also means that more weeds are growing in the hot, dry weather. They take nutrients and water away from the plants we grow for food.

HOW SEEDS MOVE (AND WHY THEY NEED TO)

Seeds must move away from their parent plants or they might not grow. If all seeds just fell to the ground beneath the plants they came from, they would have a tough time competing with their parent plants for food, water, sunlight and space. They might not germinate, and if they did, their chances of survival would be slim. But how do seeds move away from their parent plants when they can't simply get up and walk away?

Seeds get around in some clever ways. This movement is called *dispersal*. One of the most common types of seed dispersal occurs when wildlife or birds eat the seeds or fruit containing the seeds and then deposit those seeds somewhere else in their droppings. In the same way, *carnivorous* animals such as coyotes, wolves and cougars might eat other small mammals such as mice and squirrels, and pass along the seeds that the smaller animals ate.

Wildlife and birds also get some kinds of sticky seeds, or *burrs*, caught in their fur or feathers. The seeds are dropped in a different location when the animals clean themselves or shed their fur or feathers. (Humans can carry seeds this way too! Have you ever been on a hike and brought back burs on your socks or pants?)

Plants Need to Adapt

Due to the climate crisis, plants will need to adapt to changing temperatures and find different sources of water, which means they might not be able to grow in the same places they once did. They will need to move to other locations or ranges to be able to survive. Wildlife and birds could help disperse seeds to ranges with better climates, where they could grow. It is estimated that half of the world's plants rely on animals for seed dispersal. But animals will be

Spotted lanternflies suck the sap out of tree trunks and branches.
AMY LUTZ/SHUTTERSTOCK.COM

Burdock is full of prickly seeds that can be spread around easily by wildlife or humans.
KATERYNA PUCHKA/SHUTTERSTOCK.COM

affected by the climate crisis too. If there aren't enough animals to help with seed dispersal, plants won't be able to change ranges. The plant species will be unable to adapt and will die out.

DROPPING SEEDS WITH DRONES

Since 2020, in the traditional territory of the Gitxsan Nation in northern British Columbia, developer Natasha Kuperman has led a special project called Seed the North. The 13,514-square-mile (35,000-square-kilometer) area has been logged in the past and has also experienced natural disasters such as flooding. It is difficult to plant new trees in this area because it is so hard to get to it. But it's important to reforest the land and restore a healthy ecosystem. The Indigenous people in the area trap and hunt for food. Restoring the forest means that wildlife will have a place to live, eat and raise their young. Reforestation projects undertaken by the forest industry usually plant only one or two species of trees, but Seed the North sows many types of tree seeds to promote biodiversity.

To give the seeds their best chance of germinating, they are coated in a material called biochar. Biochar is

Sow Deeper: Some Seeds Fly, Explode, Float or Burn!

Maple trees have beautiful winged seeds called *samaras*. Their little helicopter-like blades help the wind carry them to new places. Other plants have an explosive way of making their seeds move. Some plants, such as lentils, have seed pods that burst open when the seeds and the pods are ripe. The seeds then fly all over the place. Sometimes seeds are dispersed by water. In tropical countries, coconuts fall off the tree, land in nearby water and float to a new home somewhere else. Seeds can also be dispersed by fire, but in this case, the seeds don't travel. They simply must survive the fire. These types of seeds—such as those from lodgepole pines—contain a type of resin or glue that melts in high heat. The seed is dormant, or asleep, until the melting wakes it up. It then germinates in the newly burned land.

28

It's easy to figure out how these thistle seeds get around!
SHERYL NORMANDEAU

like charcoal. It is made from plant matter such as grass and the short stalks left over when a grain crop is harvested. The biochar coating helps prevent the seeds from drying out, so they are more likely to sprout. (Remember, seeds need water to germinate.) The biochar also tastes bad to most animals, which helps ensure that the seeds will stay where they are sown. Seed the North uses drones to drop tree seeds over the hard-to-reach area. Drones can fly long distances, and they don't cost a lot to fly. Seed the North is trying to regrow forests in a way that is respectful of the environment and the people who live there.

POLLINATION PROBLEMS

Have you ever watched a bumblebee as it buzzes around a flower? If you look closely, you might see the sticky grains of pollen it carries on its pollen basket, or corbicula. It has one on each hind leg. Pollen helps a plant make seeds. For this to happen, pollen must get from the male part of a flower to the female part of the flower. Many plants are insect-pollinated, which is where the bee comes in.

Flower Parts

Some flowers have both male and female parts. Others have separate male flowers and female flowers. The pollen must move from

Squash plants, such as this zucchini, have separate male and female flowers on the same plant. If you look at this photo, the male flowers are the ones with the long straight stems. The female flowers have zucchini fruit growing from them.
SARATM/GETTY IMAGES

This beautiful (and very large!) hummingbird moth, which I photographed in the Cypress Hills of southern Alberta one summer, is also a pollinator.
SHERYL NORMANDEAU

Cones that need heat to open and release their seeds are called serotinous. The word serotiny means "later." The cones wait—sometimes for many years—until a forest fire makes them pop open.
NPS

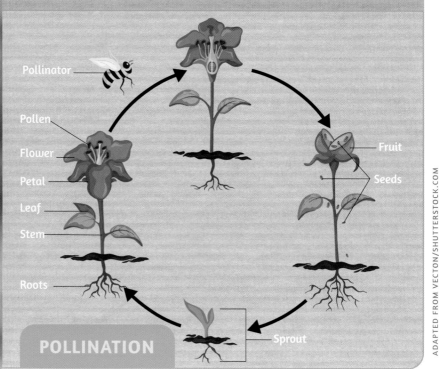

Pollinator
Pollen
Flower
Petal
Leaf
Stem
Roots
Fruit
Seeds
Sprout

POLLINATION

male parts (stamens) to female parts (pistils). The top part of the pistil is the stigma, which is where the bee lands after it has picked up its load of pollen. The pollen will be transported through the style until it reaches the ovary. Once the plant is pollinated, the ovaries become fruit. The parts called ovules that are inside the ovaries will eventually turn into seeds.

Plants such as apples and raspberries need to be *cross-pollinated* to make seeds. Insects and other pollinators such as birds help make that happen. The wind can also help with cross-pollination. It is estimated that more than 75 percent of the world's flowering plants need pollinators.

Other plants, such as tomatoes, are self-pollinated. This means that the pollen is transferred from the stamen to the pistil of the same flower. They don't absolutely need pollinators to help them, but insects and wind can help get the pollen where it needs to go.

You can see how important insects and other pollinators are to the production of seeds. If the climate crisis or pesticide use reduces the number of bees, butterflies and birds that help pollinate our plants, this will decrease our food supply. We also won't be able to use plants for medicine, fiber or building materials.

WHEN SEEDS GET SICK

Seeds can be harmed by pathogens. The pathogens may live inside the seed or on its surface. We might not be able to actually see that they are sick, but seeds infected with pathogens might not germinate and grow. If the seeds do successfully sprout, the plants that grow from them may be unhealthy. The diseases the plants get from the seeds can be passed along to other plants. This means that humans and animals who rely on the plants for food cannot eat them. When diseased seeds are stored for planting later, they can infect other seeds. When you save seeds, always pick them from plants that are healthy. This is a responsible way to be sure that pathogens do not spread into other gardens (and possibly into the wild).

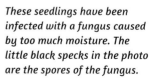

Lodgepole pines produce both serotinous and nonserotinous cones, giving the trees a greater chance of releasing seeds and having some successfully germinate and grow.
NPS/J JERRETT

These seedlings have been infected with a fungus caused by too much moisture. The little black specks in the photo are the spores of the fungus.
KOY_HIPSTER/SHUTTERSTOCK.COM

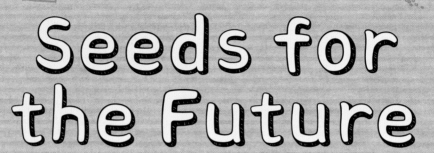

CHAPTER FOUR

Seeds for the Future

PUT IT IN THE VAULT

Growing seeds that have been collected and saved over centuries gives people of the Cherokee Nation a strong connection to their ancestors and to the land where they grow the plants.
CHEROKEE NATION COMMUNICATIONS

When you hear the words *vault* and *bank*, what comes to mind? Money, right? Even though a lot of our money is electronic these days, banks and vaults still store some paper money and coins. They keep our funds safe so that we can use them in the future. Seed banks do a similar thing. These special places have been built to store seeds from plants from all over the world. The seeds are protected so that they will be ready for use in case the plant goes extinct.

TYPES OF SEED BANKS

Seed banks are often owned by a group of nations working together to collect seeds, deposit them in the seed banks and ensure that the banks are organized and maintained. A seed bank must be protected against extreme weather or natural

These seed samples are stored in a plant-gene bank. They are used by scientists to help breed new plants. The new plants will have desirable traits, such as better resistance to pests and diseases or the ability to withstand colder temperatures.

disasters that could destroy the building and against people who might try to take control of the seeds during times of war.

There are around 1,400 seed banks in the world. One of the most well-known seed banks in the world belongs to the Cherokee Nation in Tahlequah, Oklahoma. This is the first Indigenous nation to collect and store seeds in its own seed bank. It preserves plants that have been part of Cherokee heritage for thousands of years, including tobacco and several varieties of corn, beans and squash. Each year more than 20 varieties of seeds are collected by and shared with members of the Cherokee Nation.

Navdanya is a group founded by Dr. Vandana Shiva, in Uttarakhand, India. Shiva and her colleages work with farmers in India and have preserved more than 7,000 different crop varieties. There are 150 community seed banks across India operated by Navdanya and managed by the farming communities.

The Seed Savers Exchange was started in the United States in 1975. It banks heirloom seeds that were brought to North America by immigrants from all over the world. Seeds of Diversity is a Canadian organization with over 1,000 members who work together to save seeds and build biodiversity.

Sow Deeper: How Long Do Seeds Live?

Seeds are only viable for a certain length of time. *Viability* is a seed's ability to germinate and grow into a plant. The seeds need the right temperature and enough water and oxygen to sprout. If seeds are too old or not stored properly, they might not germinate and grow. Every plant seed has its own viability. Onion seeds, for example, are not viable for very long. Even if you store them in a cool, dry place, they need to be planted as soon as possible after the seeds are collected. After one year they might not sprout. Some seeds have long viability. Seeds from cucumbers, lettuce and celery can be viable for up to five years or longer.

The seeds from this beautiful Flashy Trout Back heirloom lettuce will be viable for many years.
DANITA DELIMONT/SHUTTERSTOCK.COM

Rows and rows of bins filled with seeds are kept inside the temperature-controlled Svalbard Global Seed Vault.
NORDGEN/DAG TERJE FILIP ENDRESEN/
WIKIMEDIA COMMONS/PUBLIC DOMAIN

In 2013 Chinese researchers were able to germinate a 1,300-year-old seed from a lotus plant. Now that's a seed with a long viability! In the world's seed banks, scientists store all the seeds at the optimum temperature and in special containers to keep the seeds viable. New seeds are frequently brought into the seed banks to keep the inventory fresh and replenished.

THE OLDEST SEED VAULT IN THE WORLD

In 1941, during World War II, the German army invaded the Russian city of Leningrad (now St. Petersburg). Two million people lived in the city at the time, and the siege—which lasted for nearly three years—prevented them from getting food. More than one million people died, including a group of student scientists who tried to protect a massive collection of 187,000 seeds. Before the war, the members of the Institute of Plant Industry, led by Nikolai Vavilov, had collected seeds from all over the world. They hoped that by saving seeds and breeding healthy, strong plants, they could one day end world hunger. Vavilov realized that growing only a few species of crops was a

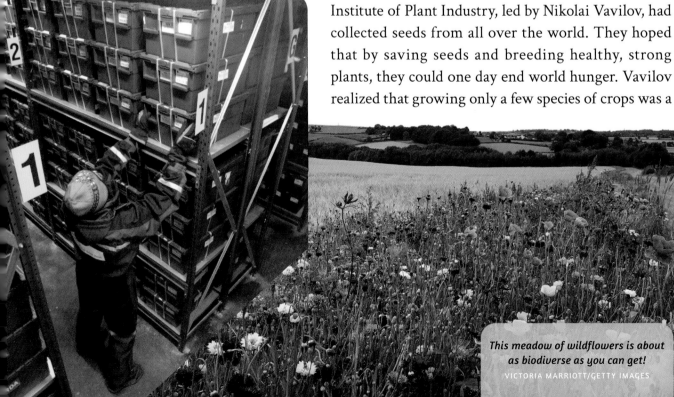

This meadow of wildflowers is about as biodiverse as you can get!
VICTORIA MARRIOTT/GETTY IMAGES

danger to biodiversity. If a nation was growing only a few types of crops and the plants were attacked by insect pests or a pathogen, the entire food supply could be wiped out. He knew that it was safer to grow a wide range of species of plants to prevent this from happening.

Even though Vavilov was imprisoned by Russian leader Josef Stalin for treason, and the nine students working on the project didn't live to see the results, many of the seeds they tried to protect survived. The plants that descended from them are grown in Russia today, and the Vavilov seed vault is still in use.

At the Vavilov Institute of Plant Industry, scientists work with seeds in the seed bank to try to breed agricultural crops that can grow well in dry climates.
STEVE RAYMER/GETTY IMAGES

The Svalbard Global Seed Vault is built into the side of Platåberget Mountain. It is a unique-looking building that was purpose-built to withstand global catastrophes, such as nuclear war and the climate crisis.
THEERASAK NAMKAMPA/SHUTTERSTOCK.COM

SVALBARD GLOBAL SEED VAULT

The Svalbard Global Seed Vault is sometimes called the "doomsday vault" because it saves seeds for future need in the event that the world, or a particular region of the world, suffers a massive catastrophe. Svalbard is a tiny archipelago off the coast of Norway. It is just over 621 miles (1,000 kilometers) from the North Pole. Svalbard is a remote place, and not very many people live there. The average high temperature during the summer months is only 44°F (7°C).

- It contains more than **A MILLION SEED** varieties.

- Each sample (package) of seeds has **500 SEEDS**.

- There are about **496 MILLION SEEDS** in the vault.

- It has room for up to **4.5 MILLION SEED SAMPLES** (that's 2.25 billion seeds!).

- **MORE THAN 90 COUNTRIES** have added seeds to the vault, including Canada, the United States, Russia, Mexico, Latvia, Indonesia, Israel, Lebanon, Greece, India, Finland, Sweden, Norway, Portugal, Taiwan, Brazil, New Zealand and many countries in Africa.

SVALBARD STATS

The Svalbard Seed Vault was built by the government of Norway and opened in 2008. It is a huge building carved 390 feet (119 meters) into the side of a mountain. Inside the vault, seeds are stored at a constant temperature of −0.4°F (−18°C). This temperature gives the seeds their best chance of staying viable. There are seeds from common crops such as wheat, rice and barley. There are also seeds from rare food and ornamental plants, including lentils, chickpeas and alfalfa varieties that were almost lost in Syria due to civil war. Each year the vault receives deposits of seeds from around the world. Only the organizations and countries that deposit the seeds can take them out again in the future if they are needed.

TAKE ACTION: WE CAN ALL SAVE SEEDS!

It doesn't matter if you grow one tomato plant in a pot or a whole garden full of vegetables—you can save seeds (or start your own seed vault). It's easy to do, and if you store them properly, you can plant them next year. Then you can save more seeds and start the cycle all over again!

PEAS, BEANS
AND OTHER PLANTS WITH SEED PODS

1. After the plants flower, they will form seed pods. Let some of the seed pods dry out on the plant. This could take until the end of the growing season. You'll know they're dry if the seeds inside rattle when you shake the pods. The seed pods will also turn brown.
2. Pick the seed pods off the plant and open them to see the seeds inside.

SPINACH, DILL
AND OTHER PLANTS WITHOUT SEED PODS

1. Leave some of the dried flowers on the stems. The seeds will form inside the dried flowers. Let the seeds dry out on the plants. They will feel hard.
2. Remove the stems that hold the seeds from the plant. Pull all the seeds away from the flowers. (If the seeds are small, put the flower stems inside a paper bag. You can catch the seeds in the bag when you pull them off the stems.)

TOMATOES

1. When you scoop out the seeds from a tomato, you'll notice that they are covered in a jellylike goo. That goo contains abscisic acid, which helps keep the seeds from sprouting inside the tomatoes.
2. Put the tomato seeds and pulp into a glass jar. Add water to fully cover. Let the jar sit in a warm place (but not in direct sunlight!) for two or three days. Stir the mixture once a day. Put the seeds in a strainer to drain the liquid and then rinse the seeds. Dry them on a piece of baking parchment paper.

PUMPKINS, ZUCCHINI
AND OTHER TYPES OF SQUASH

1. Get an adult to help you cut open the squash fruit. Scoop out the seeds. If there is any gloopy pulp sticking to the seeds, wash it off.
2. Pat the seeds dry with a towel.
3. Evenly spread the seeds on a cookie sheet lined with baking parchment paper.
4. Put the cookie sheet in a cool, dry place. Let the seeds dry out for a month.

STORING SEEDS

No matter which type of seeds you save, you must store them properly so they can be used in the future. Seeds that rot will not sprout!

1. Be sure your seeds are completely dry before you store them.
2. Put your seeds into paper envelopes or brown paper bags. Seal them so the seeds don't fall out.
3. Label your seed packages with the name of the plant and the date you collected the seeds. You can also add information like *Tomato fruit was red and the size of a golf ball* or *Sweet pea flowers were pale pink and smelled really good*. This will help you remember what traits you liked about the plants you got the seeds from.
4. Put the seed packages in a cool, dry place with a consistent temperature. The seeds must not get wet.

If you wait until just the right time to collect seeds, they won't become moldy. For seeds that need to be collected when they are dry, you shouldn't see any green on the stems, the seed heads or the seeds themselves. Everything should be brown before you pick the seeds.
HMVART/GETTY IMAGES

INSTEAD OF BOOKS, CHECK OUT SOME SEEDS!

Seed libraries are popping up all over the world. You don't borrow books at seed libraries—you borrow seeds to plant in your own garden. At the end of the season you save seeds from the plants you have grown and return packages of seeds to the library. This is a way for gardeners like you to keep sharing parts of your gardens with others.

The Edmonton Public Library set up a seed library at one of its branches in 2022. Patrons can "check out" up to 10 varieties of seeds from plants such as peas, beans and carrots and then plant them in their own gardens. The library encourages anyone who gets seeds from the library to save them at the end of the season and bring some back to the library.

In 2010 there were very few seed libraries at public libraries in the United States, but thanks to a program started by science teacher Rebecca Newman in California, over 500 seed library programs were set up in public libraries across the country in just 10 years.

Shelby Montgomery, the founder of the Calgary Seed Library, says that when we plant and collect seeds, we learn lessons about the cycles in nature. We also learn where our food comes from. This can inspire us to take care of our communities and the many species that live around us.
CALGARY SEED LIBRARY

LITTLE FREE SEED LIBRARIES

Have you ever walked by a house on a city street and found a Little Free Library in the front yard? It's where people drop off books they've read and take other books in exchange. Some people have built Little Seed Libraries where gardeners can exchange seeds. People grow plants from the seeds, save the seeds and then bring the new seeds back to the library to share.

Laurel Malialis built a Little Free Seed Library in her front-yard garden in Calgary. She says it's been well received by the community. "I share when seeds are added on Facebook, and neighbors often stop in to check the box," she said. "Sometimes if people are looking for specific seeds, they will message me, and I'll leave them in our mailbox." She also stocks the library with beginner and familiar seeds for plants such as sunflowers and beans.

SHARING THE BOUNTY

People are swapping seeds online too. It is easy to organize trades and exchange information. I run a seed-swap group on Facebook that people from my home province of Alberta can join. They post about seeds they have available for other gardeners or ask for seeds they want to plant in their gardens. Members of the group send out self-addressed, stamped envelopes (SASEs) to get the seeds they want from others.

Seed swapping is a fun way to increase the diversity of your garden and help others do the same. You can meet gardeners from all over your province, state or country. Make sure it's okay with your parents for you to swap seeds online. Ask them to help you make SASEs to send and receive seeds.

FACT

Check your federal government's regulations for swapping seeds with people from other countries. It may require a permit. This information is typically available online.

Let's Celebrate Seeds!

National Seed Swap Day in the United States has been held annually on the last Saturday of January since 2006. It's a day for gardeners to celebrate seeds from their own gardens and share those seeds with others. It's a good way to prepare for the upcoming spring planting season.

International Seeds Day is held every year on April 26. This is a day to remind people why seeds are so important. It is also a day to learn more about the importance of organic farming and the rights of farmers, particularly in developing countries. On International Seeds Day—and every day!—think about how seeds can be protected and saved for the future.

Sharing seeds with members of a community garden can benefit many people!
SHERYL NORMANDEAU

COMMUNITY SPIRIT

Many towns and cities have community gardens. They can be found in parks, near community centers or apartment complexes, or attached to seniors' homes and churches. People from the community pay money to rent a plot in the garden for the year. They can then grow plants there. Sometimes the gardeners use the bounty from the plants themselves, and other times they donate vegetables and fruit to food banks. Community gardeners love to receive and share seeds. You could give some of your extra seeds to them—and you will probably get some in return!

THE STORY OF SEEDY SATURDAY

In March 1990 a special seed-sharing event was held in Vancouver, British Columbia. It was the first Seedy Saturday. Today hundreds of Seedy Saturday (or Sunday) events take place all over North America. They provide a chance for gardeners of all ages to get together to buy, sell and swap seeds. At some events expert gardeners

Be a Citizen Scientist!

I live a few hours away from beautiful Waterton Lakes National Park in Alberta. One day, on social media, I saw a call for volunteers. Parks Canada, which looks after Waterton, needed people to go to the park and help collect seeds from a few plant species. My brother and I signed up to help. We joined a group led by a Parks employee and picked the seeds of a type of spear grass that grows in the area, as well as a wildflower called Drummond's mountain-avens. We wore big canvas-and-leather bags around our waists and stuffed the seeds inside. Afterward the seeds were taken to a special facility where staff properly dried and stored them. The avens seeds we collected will be planted in an area of the park with abandoned gravel pits. In a few years' time the area will be filled with beautiful flowers that pollinators love.

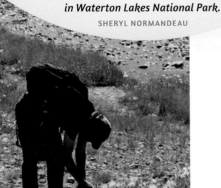

My brother, Derek, collects avens seeds in Waterton Lakes National Park.
SHERYL NORMANDEAU

and people who work in the horticultural industry give talks about topics such as seed saving. Seedy Saturday is a time to celebrate planting and saving seeds and sharing them with others. In Canada, you can look at the Seeds of Diversity website to find out where and when Seedy Saturday events will be held in your area. Don't forget to take some of the seeds you've saved from your garden to trade with other people.

WE ALL NEED SEEDS

There are many reasons why we need to save seeds. Without plants, we can't meet many of our basic needs, like food, shelter, clothing and medicine. Seeds also have stories and are reminders of the people who lived before us, who planted crops and gathered the harvest.

When you are working in your garden or walking in a field of wildflowers, look around you. Do you see pollinators interacting with the plants? Is the wind blowing seeds around? Are there birds gobbling up seeds or berries? I hope so!

TEDDI YAEGER PHOTOGRAPHY/GETTY IMAGES

Acknowledgments

I'd like to extend a thank-you to the incredible team at Orca Book Publishers. The opportunity to write this book is a dream come true!

Huge appreciation to Tina Boisvert and Rob Normandeau for contributing photographs to the book.

A million thanks to Shelby Montgomery and the team at the Calgary Seed Library—I am so grateful for Shelby's time and insight into this forward-thinking, hugely inspiring seed-saving venture.

Tons of gratitude to Laurel Malialis, who didn't blink when I reached out to her on social media and asked her about her Little Free Seed Library. When I stopped by to see her delightful garden, it was filled with the buzzing of bees hard at work.

ALI MAJDFAR/GETTY IMAGES

Resources

Print

Bone, Emily. *It All Starts with a Seed: How Food Grows.* Usborne Publishing, 2017.

Buchanan, Shelly C. *Plant Reproduction.* Teacher Created Materials, 2016.

Castaldo, Nancy F. *The Story of Seeds: From Mendel's Garden to Your Plate, and How There's More of Less to Eat Around the World.* Houghton Mifflin Harcourt, 2016.

Jacobs, Pat. *Why Do Plants Have Flowers? And Other Questions About Evolution and Classification.* PowerKids Press, 2017.

Juettner, Bonnie. *The Seed Vault.* Norwood House Press, 2009.

Morgan, Sally. *Discover It Yourself: Plants and Flowers.* Kingfisher, 2022.

Orme, Helen. *Seeds, Bulbs, Plants, and Flowers* (part of the Science Everywhere! series). New Forest Press, 2010.

Royston, Angela. *What Do You Know About Plants?* PowerKids Press, 2018.

Stewart, Melissa. *A Seed Is the Start.* National Geographic Kids, 2018.

Stewart, Melissa. *How Does a Seed Sprout? And Other Questions About Plants.* Sterling Children's Books, 2014.

Online

Pollinator Partnership: pollinator.org
Seeds of Diversity Canada: seeds.ca
Svalbard Global Seed Bank: seedvault.nordgen.org

Videos

"How Does a Seed Become a Plant?" and "How Do Plant Seeds Travel?" by SciShow Kids, YouTube: youtube.com/ @SciShowKids

"Let's Save the Pollinators," by Varun Valentine, TEDx Talk: ted.com/talks/varun_valentine_let_s_ save_the_pollinators

"Why is biodiversity so important?" by Kim Preshoff, TED-Ed video: ed.ted.com/lessons/why-is-biodiversity- so-important-kim-preshoff

Glossary

biodiversity—the variety of animal and plant life in an environment

burrs—rough, prickly coverings on the seeds of some plants that make them stick to things they come in contact with

carnivorous—feeding mostly on animal meat

clones—plants that are genetically identical to their parent plant

crossbreeding—mixing two varieties of plants within the same species to produce traits, such as better flavor or prettier color

cross-pollinated—pollinated by transferring pollen from one plant to another

dispersal—movement from one place to another

embryo—egg

endosperm—part of a seed that provides food for the plant's embryo

fertilized—pollen from the male flower has reached the egg of the female flower

genetic engineering—using technology to change the genetic material of a plant

genetics—the study of characteristics that are passed down from one generation of a living organism to another

germinate—to sprout

heirloom—a plant variety that has been passed down for generations

horticultural—pertaining to the science and art of growing plants

hybrid—a plant produced by two different species of plants

invasive—(of a species) tending to spread quickly and aggressively in an area where it is not wanted or not native

kingdoms—in the classification of living things, one of the main categories that organisms are divided into based on their characteristics

native—living or growing naturally in a certain region

patent—to obtain the exclusive legal right to make, use or sell something, including a plant breeder's creation

pathogens—things that cause disease, such as a fungus, virus or bacterium

petri dish—a small shallow bowl used to grow cells and tissue cultures of organisms in a laboratory

pollinated—pollen has been transferred from a male flower part to a female flower part

selective breeding—choosing particular parent plants and breeding them together to create offspring that have desirable traits

sexual reproduction—reproduction of plants by seeds

status symbols—possessions that show a person's wealth or place in society

testa—the coating on the outside of a seed

trait—an inherited characteristic

viability—the ability of a seed to germinate and grow into a mature plant under the right conditions

Index

Page numbers in **bold** indicate an image caption.

RANDAL ALLCOCK

SHERYL NORMANDEAU is a lifelong gardener and holds a Prairie Horticulture Certificate and a Sustainable Urban Agriculture Certificate. She is a freelance writer specializing in gardening writing, with hundreds of articles published. She is a regular contributor to *Herb Quarterly, Gardener for Canadian Climates* and *Prairie Garden,* and the author of *The Little Prairie Book of Berries.* Sheryl lives in Calgary.